Dreamer's

J O U R N A L

Paula

PUBLISHED BY

BRONZE
BOW PUB.

Copyright © 2005 by Paula White

All rights reserved. No part of this publication can be reproduced, stored in a
retrievable system, or transmitted, in any form or by any means electronic,
mechanical, photocopying, recording, or otherwise, except by the inclusion of
brief quotations in a review, without prior permission in writing from the
Publisher.

All Scriptures are taken from the New King James Version. Copyright © 1982
by Thomas Nelson, Inc. Used by permission. All rights reserved.

Published by Bronze Bow Publishing, Inc. and Paula White Ministries.

Bronze Bow Publishing Inc.,
2600 E. 26th Street, Minneapolis, MN 55406

You can reach Bronze Bow Publishing on the Internet at
www.bronzebowpublishing.com.

Paula White Ministries
P.O. Box 25151
Tampa, Florida 33622

ISBN 1-932458-38-7

You can reach Paula White Ministries on the Internet at www.paulawhite.org.

Literary development and cover/interior design by Koechel Peterson &
Associates, Inc., Minneapolis, Minnesota.

Manufactured in Hong Kong

"ALL THINGS ARE POSSIBLE
TO HIM WHO BELIEVES."

MARK 9:23

Introduction

I AM EXCITED that you have taken the initiative to purposefully
and passionately pursue your dreams. I prayed that God would
send the right people for whom this journal is designed . . . indi-
viduals who know that greatness lies within them. You are it!
You are chosen and set apart.

I DARE YOU TO DREAM! History makers and world changers
are men and women who dreamed of a world beyond its cur-
rent state. Everything begins with an idea, a wish, a dream.
Think big! Dream beyond your own capabilities. Think outside
the box. At times your dream and vision may seem so big that it
overwhelms you, but chase after it! Overtake it! Capture it!

YOUR DREAM is your most valuable possession. It belongs to you
and to no one else. You can't live your life through someone else,
and you can't live your life for someone else. No one can take your
dream unless you give it away. Like a child, your dream needs to

be nurtured, exercised, directed, and protected. Your dream will stretch you, challenge you, frustrate you, and reward you.

YOUR BELIEF ABOUT YOURSELF is inextricably tied to what you will achieve in life. Your unique way of thinking is what separates you from others. Don't allow past mistakes or the fear of failure or the fear of success to stand between you and your dream. And don't allow anyone to minimize your dream, and never entrust your dream to just anyone. If they can't rejoice over it, don't share it with them. If they can't encourage, promote, or help cultivate your dream, keep it between you and God. Don't allow yourself to become sidetracked. Stay focused on your dream.

IF YOU DON'T LIKE where you are, if you don't like the opportunities you have, if you don't like your environment, then change your thinking. If you don't change your thinking, you can hold a diamond and not see its brilliance; you can inherit millions and still feel poverty-stricken. Activate the Word of God in your life so that your mind will be renewed and transformed. Rid yourself of negative self-talk and toss out the negative messages that life has hurled at you.

IN THIS JOURNAL, I hope that you'll take the opportunity to consider your dreams in the light of God's Word. What discoveries are you making about your dreams? What are the dreams that you believe God has put in your heart? What can you do to make your dreams happen? Your daily reflections will tell the story.

RISE UP, DREAMER! Shake off the chains that hold you back, and become a prisoner of hope (Zechariah 9:12 paraphrased).

Why Journal?

IF YOU HAVE EVER DOUBTED the importance and value of
keeping a journal, you need look no further than the New
Testament. Its pages are filled with journal entries projecting
the lives and experiences of men and women like you and me.
Through their writings, we get a close-up and personal experi-
ence of their triumphs and pain. But most importantly, their
writings provide a manuscript through which we can know the
ways of God, hear His voice, and put into practice the teachings
of Christ.

YOUR WALK WITH GOD and your personal dreams for your life
deserve the same attention. Use these pages to freely express
your thoughts as your dream grows from idea to reality—
whether it regards your career, your relationship with your

spouse or children, your spiritual life, your finances, your health and fitness, your friendships, or whatever. It is important that you express what is truly in your heart. Be authentically you.

JOURNALING IS AN EXERCISE that has enhanced my faith walk and has revealed God's faithfulness in my life as I have learned to trust Him. It has created a lasting record of my conversations with God. In the stillness and sanctity of my journal time, God's voice is loudest in my life. It's through my volumes and volumes of journals that I have found a lasting record of my friendship with God.

I WISH the very same for you.

Paula

How to Use this Journal

I'VE ALWAYS KEPT A JOURNAL, and I have cherished the privilege of speaking directly to God through prayer since the day I put my faith in Jesus Christ. So prayer journaling, in particular, came quite naturally to me. What I didn't know early on was that I would actually be able to have conversations with God, to talk to and hear back from Him. The beautiful poetic language of the King James Bible intimidated me. I thought I had to speak to God in the language of Abraham or David. Not so.

WHEN YOU SPEAK TO GOD, it does not have to be formal. James 2:23 says that because Abraham believed in God, he was a friend of God. Do you believe in God? Well, then you, too, are His friend. Formalities such as *thee* and *thou* can be put aside for casual terms of endearment such as *Daddy* and *Father*. He just wants to hear from you. Speak to Him from your heart, and He will speak to you from His.

DEDICATING A "JOURNAL TIME" each day will help you to get into the routine of journaling. Choose a quiet, private place to shut out the cares of the world and steal away with God. Perhaps a good time for you is just before retiring for the evening or in the morning before the rest of your family awakes. It may help to play soothing worship music to calm your mind and quiet the distractions of the day.

BE SURE TO NOTATE the date at the beginning of each entry. This will be particularly interesting to you as you reflect back over the pages later on. Then check the box that best describes your journal entry for the day. Are you expressing the obstacles or challenges you are facing in achieving your dreams? Are you recording what you believe God is challenging you to do to make your dreams come true? Take as much space as you need to jot down whatever you feel or are thinking, running into several pages if necessary. Allow yourself to flow freely, releasing any tensions, anxieties, or worries to God through your pen. Talk to Him, listen to Him, commune with Him. The more often you do it, the more natural it will feel.

HABAKKUK 2:2 encourages us to "write the vision and make it plain on tablets, that he may run who reads it." Periodically throughout this journal, you will find "Reflections" pages. These pages are intended to give you an opportunity to review several entries at a time so that you can see your own personal growth and to remind you of the desires you have written. They also provide you the opportunity to reflect on all that God has spoken to you and performed in your life. Take every opportunity to appreciate the smallest answered prayer and to meditate on God's faithfulness.

Date

○ _Today's opportunities and challenges . . ._

   ○ _To transform my dream into reality, I need to . . ._

To hold on to your dream and fulfill God's plan for your life, you must keep moving forward.

Date

○ Today's opportunities and challenges . . .

   ○ To transform my dream into reality, I need to . . .

"FOR YOU ARE A
HOLY PEOPLE TO
THE LORD YOUR
GOD; THE LORD
YOUR GOD HAS
CHOSEN YOU TO BE
A PEOPLE FOR
HIMSELF, A SPECIAL
TREASURE ABOVE
ALL THE PEOPLES
ON THE FACE OF
THE EARTH."

DEUTERONOMY 7:6

Date

○ Today's opportunities and challenges . . .

    ○ To transform my dream into reality, I need to . . .

Give yourself a picture of your potential.

Date

○ Today's opportunities and challenges . . .

   ○ To transform my dream into reality, I need to . . .

"BUT THOSE WHO
WAIT ON THE
LORD SHALL
RENEW THEIR
STRENGTH; THEY
SHALL MOUNT UP
WITH WINGS LIKE
EAGLES, THEY
SHALL RUN AND
NOT BE WEARY,
THEY SHALL WALK
AND NOT FAINT."

ISAIAH 40:31

Date

○ Today's opportunities and challenges . . .
  ○ To transform my dream into reality, I need to . . .

As long as you don't quit, you will never lose.

Date

○ Today's opportunities and challenges . . .

   ○ To transform my dream into reality, I need to . . .

THEN DAVID SAID
[GOLIATH], "YOU
COME TO ME WITH
A SWORD, WITH A
SPEAR, AND WITH
A JAVELIN. BUT I
COME TO YOU IN
THE NAME OF THE
LORD OF HOSTS,
THE GOD OF THE
ARMIES OF ISRAEL,
WHOM YOU HAVE
DEFIED. THIS DAY
THE LORD WILL
DELIVER YOU INTO
MY HAND, AND I
WILL STRIKE YOU
AND TAKE YOUR
HEAD FROM YOU."

1 SAMUEL 17:45–46

Date

○ *Today's opportunities and challenges . . .*

   ○ *To transform my dream into reality, I need to . . .*

Motivation is deeper than words. Motives have a lot to do with who you are.

○ Today's opportunities and challenges . . .

    ○ To transform my dream into reality, I need to . . .

FOR HE WHO SOWS
TO HIS FLESH WILL
OF THE FLESH REAP
CORRUPTION, BUT
HE WHO SOWS TO
THE SPIRIT WILL
OF THE SPIRIT
REAP EVERLASTING
LIFE. AND LET US
NOT GROW WEARY
WHILE DOING
GOOD, FOR IN DUE
SEASON WE SHALL
REAP IF WE DO
NOT LOSE HEART.

GALATIANS 6:8–9

Date

○ Today's opportunities and challenges . . .

  ○ To transform my dream into reality, I need to . . .

"Success" only comes before "work" in the dictionary.

Date

○ *Today's opportunities and challenges . . .*

○ *To transform my dream into reality, I need to . . .*

....
....
....
....
....
....
....
....

A person with a past can touch a God in the present who is able to change the future.

....
....
....
....
....
....
....
....
....
....
....

○ Today's opportunities and challenges . . .

   ○ To transform my dream into reality, I need to . . .

"A LITTLE ONE
SHALL BECOME A
THOUSAND, AND A
SMALL ONE A
STRONG NATION. I,
THE LORD, WILL
HASTEN IT IN ITS
TIME."

ISAIAH 60:22

Date

○ *Today's opportunities and challenges . . .*

  ○ *To transform my dream into reality, I need to . . .*

Don't despise small beginnings—they can turn into large endings.

Date

○ Today's opportunities and challenges . . .

   ○ To transform my dream into reality, I need to . . .

IN GOD (I WILL
PRAISE HIS WORD),
IN THE LORD
(I WILL PRAISE
HIS WORD), IN
GOD I HAVE PUT
MY TRUST; I WILL
NOT BE AFRAID.
WHAT CAN MAN
DO TO ME?

PSALM 56:10–11

Date

○ *Today's opportunities and challenges . . .*

    ○ *To transform my dream into reality, I need to . . .*

When you know who you are, you don't have to struggle to live up to what someone has defined you to be.

Date

○ *Today's opportunities and challenges . . .*

    ○ *To transform my dream into reality, I need to . . .*

"AGAIN, THE
KINGDOM OF
HEAVEN IS LIKE
TREASURE HIDDEN
IN A FIELD,
WHICH A MAN
FOUND AND HID;
AND FOR JOY
OVER IT HE GOES
AND SELLS ALL
THAT HE HAS AND
BUYS THAT FIELD."

MATTHEW 13:44

○ Today's opportunities and challenges . . .

   ○ To transform my dream into reality, I need to . . .

For any new level in life, there is a "cost of admission"—pay the price.

Reflections 1

JUST AS A GREAT OAK TREE began with a single acorn, so any achievement we make in life begins with a dream. No matter what your age or condition, God has given you dreams that He longs to see fulfilled in your life. Because of His great love, you can trust Him to bring them to pass.

TAKE TIME TO REVIEW the last several pages of this journal. Reflect on all the things you have discovered about your dreams. As you've thought about your dreams in the light of God's Word, what are you learning? Are there specific dreams that you believe God wants you to focus upon? What can you do to make your dreams come true?

CAPTURE your thoughts below.

_____

_____

_____

_____

_____

_____

_____

_____

Date

Date

○ *Today's opportunities and challenges . . .*

  ○ *To transform my dream into reality, I need to . . .*

"ASSUREDLY,
I SAY TO YOU,
WHATEVER YOU
BIND ON EARTH
WILL BE BOUND
IN HEAVEN, AND
WHATEVER YOU
LOOSE ON
EARTH WILL BE
LOOSED IN
HEAVEN."

MATTHEW 18:18

Date

○ *Today's opportunities and challenges . . .*

    ○ *To transform my dream into reality, I need to . . .*

If opportunity doesn't knock, then build a door.

○ *Today's opportunities and challenges . . .*

   ○ *To transform my dream into reality, I need to . . .*

AND MY GOD
SHALL SUPPLY ALL
YOUR NEED
ACCORDING TO
HIS RICHES IN
GLORY BY CHRIST
JESUS.

PHILIPPIANS 4:19

Date

○ *Today's opportunities and challenges . . .*

    ○ *To transform my dream into reality, I need to . . .*

Your greatest weaknesses will stop your greatest desires.

Date

○ *Today's opportunities and challenges . . .*

    ○ *To transform my dream into reality, I need to . . .*

FOR GOD HAS NOT
GIVEN US A SPIRIT
OF FEAR, BUT OF
POWER AND OF
LOVE AND OF A
SOUND MIND.

2 TIMOTHY 1:7

○ Today's opportunities and challenges . . .

　　○ To transform my dream into reality, I need to . . .

Recognize that those who reject you have no ability to see inside you.

Date

○ *Today's opportunities and challenges . . .*

   ○ *To transform my dream into reality, I need to . . .*

LET THEM SHOUT
FOR JOY AND BE
GLAD, WHO FAVOR MY
RIGHTEOUS CAUSE;
AND LET THEM SAY
CONTINUALLY, "LET
THE LORD BE
MAGNIFIED, WHO HAS
PLEASURE IN THE
PROSPERITY OF HIS
SERVANT."

PSALM 35:27

Date

○ Today's opportunities and challenges . . .

   ○ To transform my dream into reality, I need to . . .

Some of the people who fight you are preparing you for where you're going.

Date

○ *Today's opportunities and challenges . . .*

○ *To transform my dream into reality, I need to . . .*

AND WHAT MORE SHALL I SAY? FOR THE TIME WOULD FAIL
ME TO TELL OF GIDEON AND BARAK AND SAMSON AND
JEPHTHAH, ALSO OF DAVID AND SAMUEL AND THE
PROPHETS: WHO THROUGH FAITH SUBDUED KINGDOMS,
WORKED RIGHTEOUSNESS, OBTAINED PROMISES, STOPPED
THE MOUTHS OF LIONS, QUENCHED THE VIOLENCE OF FIRE,
ESCAPED THE EDGE OF THE SWORD, OUT OF WEAKNESS WERE
MADE STRONG, BECAME VALIANT IN BATTLE, TURNED TO
FLIGHT THE ARMIES OF THE ALIENS. WOMEN RECEIVED
THEIR DEAD RAISED TO LIFE AGAIN.

HEBREWS 11:32–35

Date

○ *Today's opportunities and challenges . . .*

○ *To transform my dream into reality, I need to . . .*

THE LORD MY GOD
WILL ENLIGHTEN MY
DARKNESS. FOR BY
YOU I CAN RUN
AGAINST A TROOP, BY
MY GOD I CAN LEAP
OVER A WALL. AS FOR
GOD, HIS WAY IS
PERFECT; THE WORD
OF THE LORD IS
PROVEN; HE IS A
SHIELD TO ALL WHO
TRUST IN HIM.

PSALM 18:28–30

Date

○ *Today's opportunities and challenges . . .*

   ○ *To transform my dream into reality, I need to . . .*

The door of opportunity swings on the hinges of opposition.

Date

○ _Today's opportunities and challenges . . ._

   ○ _To transform my dream into reality, I need to . . ._

GIVE US HELP
FROM TROUBLE,
FOR THE HELP OF
MAN IS USELESS.
THROUGH GOD
WE WILL DO
VALIANTLY, FOR IT
IS HE WHO SHALL
TREAD DOWN OUR
ENEMIES.

PSALM 108:12–13

$\mathcal{D}_{ate}$ ....

○ Today's opportunities and challenges . . .

   ○ To transform my dream into reality, I need to . . .

_____

_____

_____

_____

_____

_____

_____

People can sense when you are going somewhere, and not everyone wants
you to get there.

_____

_____

_____

_____

_____

_____

_____

_____

_____

_____

_____

○ Today's opportunities and challenges . . .

  ○ To transform my dream into reality, I need to . . .

FOR IT IS GOD
WHO WORKS IN
YOU BOTH TO
WILL AND TO DO
FOR HIS GOOD
PLEASURE.

PHILIPPIANS 2:13

○ Date

○ Today's opportunities and challenges . . .

　　○ To transform my dream into reality, I need to . . .

You have been engineered by God to be a success.

$\mathcal{D}_{ate}$

○ Today's opportunities and challenges . . .

   ○ To transform my dream into reality, I need to . . .

"THEREFORE I SAY
TO YOU, WHATEVER
THINGS YOU ASK
WHEN YOU PRAY,
BELIEVE THAT YOU
RECEIVE THEM, AND
YOU WILL HAVE
THEM."

MARK 11:24

Date

○ *Today's opportunities and challenges . . .*

    ○ *To transform my dream into reality, I need to . . .*

Begin to exhale what God has inhaled in you.

Date

○ *Today's opportunities and challenges . . .*

   ○ *To transform my dream into reality, I need to . . .*

"BUT SEEK FIRST
THE KINGDOM OF
GOD AND HIS
RIGHTEOUSNESS,
AND ALL THESE
THINGS SHALL BE
ADDED TO YOU."

MATTHEW 6:33

Date

○ *Today's opportunities and challenges . . .*

　○ *To transform my dream into reality, I need to . . .*

You are the captain of your own vessel. You choose the direction of your life.

Date

○ Today's opportunities and challenges . . .

    ○ To transform my dream into reality, I need to . . .

Desire is a powerful motivating force. It can make you do things that you never thought you were capable of.

Date

○ *Today's opportunities and challenges . . .*

○ *To transform my dream into reality, I need to . . .*

"THEREFORE KEEP
THE WORDS OF
THIS COVENANT,
AND DO THEM,
THAT YOU MAY
PROSPER IN ALL
THAT YOU DO."

DEUTERONOMY 29:9

$Date$

○ *Today's opportunities and challenges . . .*
  ○ *To transform my dream into reality, I need to . . .*

Don't let your history hinder you from your destiny.

○ *Today's opportunities and challenges . . .*

    ○ *To transform my dream into reality, I need to . . .*

"FOR WITH GOD
NOTHING WILL BE
IMPOSSIBLE."

LUKE 1:37

Date

○ *Today's opportunities and challenges . . .*

    ○ *To transform my dream into reality, I need to . . .*

It is scientifically proven that the bumblebee cannot fly—his wingspan is too short for his body weight—but nobody ever told the bumblebee.

Date

○ Today's opportunities and challenges . . .

○ To transform my dream into reality, I need to . . .

THEN THE LORD
TURNED TO HIM
AND SAID, "GO IN
THIS MIGHT OF
YOURS, AND YOU
SHALL SAVE ISRAEL
FROM THE HAND
OF THE
MIDIANITES.
HAVE I NOT SENT
YOU?" SO HE SAID
TO HIM, "O MY
LORD, HOW CAN I
SAVE ISRAEL?
INDEED MY CLAN
IS THE WEAKEST
IN MANASSEH,
AND I AM THE
LEAST IN MY
FATHER'S HOUSE."
AND THE LORD
SAID TO HIM,
"SURELY I WILL BE
WITH YOU, AND
YOU SHALL DEFEAT
THE MIDIANITES
AS ONE MAN."

JUDGES 6:14–16

Date

○ *Today's opportunities and challenges . . .*

   ○ *To transform my dream into reality, I need to . . .*

Little people can do big things.

Date

○ *Today's opportunities and challenges . . .*

    ○ *To transform my dream into reality, I need to . . .*

HE HAS PUT A NEW SONG IN MY MOUTH—PRAISE TO
OUR GOD; MANY WILL SEE IT AND FEAR, AND WILL
TRUST IN THE LORD. BLESSED IS THAT MAN WHO MAKES
THE LORD HIS TRUST, AND DOES NOT RESPECT THE
PROUD, NOR SUCH AS TURN ASIDE TO LIES.

PSALM 40:3–4

Date

○ *Today's opportunities and challenges . . .*

   ○ *To transform my dream into reality, I need to . . .*

NOW TO HIM
WHO IS ABLE TO
DO EXCEEDINGLY
ABUNDANTLY
ABOVE ALL THAT
WE ASK OR THINK,
ACCORDING TO
THE POWER THAT
WORKS IN US, TO
HIM BE GLORY IN
THE CHURCH BY
CHRIST JESUS TO
ALL GENERATIONS,
FOREVER AND
EVER. AMEN.

EPHESIANS 3:20–21

○ *Today's opportunities and challenges . . .*

   ○ *To transform my dream into reality, I need to . . .*

*There is power working inwardly that is much greater than
anything exteriorly.*

Date

○ _Today's opportunities and challenges . . ._

    ○ _To transform my dream into reality, I need to . . ._

"IF THEY OBEY
AND SERVE HIM,
THEY SHALL SPEND
THEIR DAYS IN
PROSPERITY, AND
THEIR YEARS IN
PLEASURES."

JOB 36:11

Date

○ *Today's opportunities and challenges . . .*

   ○ *To transform my dream into reality, I need to . . .*

Never allow money to control your mission.

Date

○ *Today's opportunities and challenges . . .*

    ○ *To transform my dream into reality, I need to . . .*

COUNSEL IN THE
HEART OF MAN IS
LIKE DEEP WATER,
BUT A MAN OF
UNDERSTANDING
WILL DRAW IT OUT.

PROVERBS 20:5

Date

○ *Today's opportunities and challenges . . .*

    ○ *To transform my dream into reality, I need to . . .*

Your life will ultimately take on the direction of your thinking.

Date

○ *Today's opportunities and challenges . . .*

○ *To transform my dream into reality, I need to . . .*

HOPE DEFERRED
MAKES THE HEART
SICK, BUT WHEN
THE DESIRE COMES,
IT IS A TREE OF
LIFE.

PROVERBS 13:12

Date

○ *Today's opportunities and challenges . . .*

   ○ *To transform my dream into reality, I need to . . .*

Desire is the birthplace of productivity and fulfillment.

○ Today's opportunities and challenges . . .

　　○ To transform my dream into reality, I need to . . .

AND FROM THE
DAYS OF JOHN THE
BAPTIST UNTIL
NOW THE KING-
DOM OF HEAVEN
SUFFERS VIOLENCE,
AND THE VIOLENT
TAKE IT BY FORCE.

MATTHEW 11:12

Date

○ *Today's opportunities and challenges . . .*

　○ *To transform my dream into reality, I need to . . .*

*Passionate people find the power to push through every obstacle holding
them back.*

Date

○ *Today's opportunities and challenges . . .*

    ○ *To transform my dream into reality, I need to . . .*

BY FAITH THE WALLS
OF JERICHO FELL
DOWN AFTER THEY
WERE ENCIRCLED FOR
SEVEN DAYS. BY FAITH
THE HARLOT RAHAB
DID NOT PERISH WITH
THOSE WHO DID NOT
BELIEVE, WHEN SHE
HAD RECEIVED THE
SPIES WITH PEACE.

HEBREWS 11:30–31

Date

○ *Today's opportunities and challenges . . .*

　　○ *To transform my dream into reality, I need to . . .*

_____

_____

_____

_____

_____

_____

_____

_____

_____

_____

_____

God will cause the wall in your life to fall down, and your barrier will become your bridge.

Reflections 2

IN HEBREWS 11:8, we are told: "By faith Abraham obeyed when he was called to go out to the place which he would receive as an inheritance. And he went out, not knowing where he was going." God gave Abraham a dream, and faith took Abraham from the promise of God to the performance of it. It's always better to move in faith than to sit in doubt.

TAKE TIME TO REVIEW the last several pages of this journal. Reflect on all the things you have discovered about your dreams. As you've thought about your dreams in the light of God's Word, what are you learning? Are there specific dreams that you believe God wants you to focus upon? What can you do to make your dreams come true?

CAPTURE your thoughts below.

....

....

....

....

....

....

○ Today's opportunities and challenges . . .

　○ To transform my dream into reality, I need to . . .

SO JESUS
ANSWERED AND
SAID TO THEM,
"ASSUREDLY, I SAY
TO YOU, IF YOU
HAVE FAITH AND
DO NOT DOUBT,
YOU WILL NOT
ONLY DO WHAT
WAS DONE TO THE
FIG TREE, BUT ALSO
IF YOU SAY TO
THIS MOUNTAIN,
'BE REMOVED AND
BE CAST INTO THE
SEA,' IT WILL BE
DONE."

MATTHEW 21:21

○ Today's opportunities and challenges . . .

   ○ To transform my dream into reality, I need to . . .

Mountains don't move unless you speak to them.

○ Today's opportunities and challenges . . .

   ○ To transform my dream into reality, I need to . . .

"GIVE, AND IT
WILL BE GIVEN TO
YOU: GOOD MEAS-
URE, PRESSED
DOWN, SHAKEN
TOGETHER, AND
RUNNING OVER
WILL BE PUT INTO
YOUR BOSOM. FOR
WITH THE SAME
MEASURE THAT
YOU USE, IT WILL
BE MEASURED BACK
TO YOU."

LUKE 6:38

Date

○ *Today's opportunities and challenges . . .*

   ○ *To transform my dream into reality, I need to . . .*

Everything you need in life is within. Discover your resources
and develop them.

Date

○ Today's opportunities and challenges . . .

  ○ To transform my dream into reality, I need to . . .

THE PLANS OF THE
DILIGENT LEAD
SURELY TO PLENTY,
BUT THOSE OF
EVERYONE WHO IS
HASTY, SURELY TO
POVERTY.

PROVERBS 21:5

Date

○ *Today's opportunities and challenges . . .*

　○ *To transform my dream into reality, I need to . . .*

When you write down a goal, you increase the percentage of achieving it 90 times.

○ Today's opportunities and challenges . . .

○ To transform my dream into reality, I need to . . .

WHAT THEN SHALL
WE SAY TO THESE
THINGS? IF GOD IS
FOR US, WHO CAN BE
AGAINST US? HE
WHO DID NOT SPARE
HIS OWN SON, BUT
DELIVERED HIM UP
FOR US ALL, HOW
SHALL HE NOT WITH
HIM ALSO FREELY
GIVE US ALL THINGS?

ROMANS 8:31–32

Date

○ Today's opportunities and challenges . . .

  ○ To transform my dream into reality, I need to . . .

God is not intimidated by your aspirations. He gave them to you,
so go for it.

Date ....

○ *Today's opportunities and challenges . . .*

  ○ *To transform my dream into reality, I need to . . .*

JESUS SAID TO
HER, "DID I NOT
SAY TO YOU THAT
IF YOU WOULD
BELIEVE YOU
WOULD SEE THE
GLORY OF GOD?"

JOHN 11:40

○ *Today's opportunities and challenges . . .*

　　○ *To transform my dream into reality, I need to . . .*

Nothing big ever comes from thinking small.

○ Today's opportunities and challenges . . .

   ○ To transform my dream into reality, I need to . . .

SO JESUS STOOD
STILL AND COM-
MANDED HIM TO BE
BROUGHT TO HIM.
AND WHEN HE HAD
COME NEAR, HE
ASKED HIM, SAYING,
"WHAT DO YOU
WANT ME TO DO FOR
YOU?" HE SAID,
"LORD, THAT I MAY
RECEIVE MY SIGHT."
THEN JESUS SAID TO
HIM, "RECEIVE YOUR
SIGHT; YOUR FAITH
HAS MADE YOU
WELL."

LUKE 18:40–42

Date

○ *Today's opportunities and challenges . . .*

  ○ *To transform my dream into reality, I need to . . .*

If you really want to do something, you will find a way; if you don't, you will find an excuse.

Date

○ Today's opportunities and challenges . . .

　　○ To transform my dream into reality, I need to . . .

OH, THAT MEN
WOULD GIVE
THANKS TO THE
LORD FOR HIS
GOODNESS, AND FOR
HIS WONDERFUL
WORKS TO THE
CHILDREN OF MEN!
FOR HE SATISFIES
THE LONGING SOUL,
AND FILLS THE
HUNGRY SOUL WITH
GOODNESS."

PSALM 107:8–9

Date

○ *Today's opportunities and challenges . . .*

　○ *To transform my dream into reality, I need to . . .*

Only hungry minds can grow.

Date

○ _Today's opportunities and challenges . . ._

　○ _To transform my dream into reality, I need to . . ._

KEEP YOUR
HEART WITH ALL
DILIGENCE, FOR
OUT OF IT
SPRING THE
ISSUES OF LIFE.

PROVERBS 4:23

○ Today's opportunities and challenges . . .

    ○ To transform my dream into reality, I need to . . .

What enters your life determines what will exit.

○ *Today's opportunities and challenges . . .*

   ○ *To transform my dream into reality, I need to . . .*

AND SUDDENLY, A
WOMAN WHO HAD A
FLOW OF BLOOD FOR
TWELVE YEARS CAME
FROM BEHIND AND
TOUCHED THE HEM
OF HIS GARMENT.
FOR SHE SAID TO
HERSELF, "IF ONLY I
MAY TOUCH HIS
GARMENT, I SHALL
BE MADE WELL." BUT
JESUS TURNED
AROUND, AND WHEN
HE SAW HER HE
SAID, "BE OF GOOD
CHEER, DAUGHTER;
YOUR FAITH HAS
MADE YOU WELL."
AND THE WOMAN
WAS MADE WELL
FROM THAT HOUR.

MATTHEW 9:20–22

Date

○ Today's opportunities and challenges . . .

   ○ To transform my dream into reality, I need to . . .

Expectancy is the breeding ground for miracles.

○ Today's opportunities and challenges . . .

   ○ To transform my dream into reality, I need to . . .

FOR WE ARE HIS
WORKMANSHIP,
CREATED IN CHRIST
JESUS FOR GOOD
WORKS, WHICH
GOD PREPARED
BEFOREHAND THAT
WE SHOULD WALK
IN THEM.

EPHESIANS 2:10

Date

○ Today's opportunities and challenges . . .

    ○ To transform my dream into reality, I need to . . .

Your only boundaries in life are your own perception of potential.

Date ....

○ _Today's opportunities and challenges . . ._

　　○ _To transform my dream into reality, I need to . . ._

IF ANY OF YOU
LACKS WISDOM, LET
HIM ASK OF GOD,
WHO GIVES TO ALL
LIBERALLY AND
WITHOUT
REPROACH, AND IT
WILL BE GIVEN TO
HIM. BUT LET HIM
ASK IN FAITH, WITH
NO DOUBTING, FOR
HE WHO DOUBTS IS
LIKE A WAVE OF THE
SEA DRIVEN AND
TOSSED BY THE
WIND. FOR LET NOT
THAT MAN SUPPOSE
THAT HE WILL
RECEIVE ANYTHING
FROM THE LORD; HE
IS A DOUBLE-MIND-
ED MAN, UNSTABLE
IN ALL HIS WAYS.

JAMES 1:5–8

Date

○ *Today's opportunities and challenges . . .*

　○ *To transform my dream into reality, I need to . . .*

You cannot look ahead and look behind you at the same time.

Date

○ Today's opportunities and challenges . . .
  ○ To transform my dream into reality, I need to . . .

AND MOSES SAID
TO THE PEOPLE,
"DO NOT BE
AFRAID. STAND
STILL, AND SEE THE
SALVATION OF THE
LORD, WHICH HE
WILL ACCOMPLISH
FOR YOU TODAY.
FOR THE
EGYPTIANS WHOM
YOU SEE TODAY,
YOU SHALL SEE
AGAIN NO MORE
FOREVER. THE
LORD WILL FIGHT
FOR YOU, AND YOU
SHALL HOLD YOUR
PEACE."

EXODUS 14:13–14

Date ....

○ Today's opportunities and challenges . . .

  ○ To transform my dream into reality, I need to . . .

....

....

....

....

....

....

....

....

....

....

....

....

....

....

....

....

....

....

....

....

Your amount of success depends on the amount of adversity you can stand.

Date

○ Today's opportunities and challenges . . .

○ To transform my dream into reality, I need to . . .

"GO AND GATHER
THE ELDERS OF ISRAEL
TOGETHER, AND SAY
TO THEM, 'THE LORD
GOD OF YOUR
FATHERS, THE GOD OF
ABRAHAM, OF ISAAC,
AND OF JACOB,
APPEARED TO ME,
SAYING, "I HAVE
SURELY VISITED YOU
AND SEEN WHAT IS
DONE TO YOU IN
EGYPT; AND I HAVE
SAID I WILL BRING
YOU UP OUT OF THE
AFFLICTION OF
EGYPT TO THE LAND
OF THE CANAANITES
AND THE HITTITES
AND THE AMORITES
AND THE PERIZZITES
AND THE HIVITES
AND THE JEBUSITES,
TO A LAND FLOWING
WITH MILK AND
HONEY." ' "

EXODUS 3:16–17

○ *Today's opportunities and challenges . . .*

   ○ *To transform my dream into reality, I need to . . .*

One of your greatest gifts is the ability to see beyond where you are
right now.

Date

○ *Today's opportunities and challenges . . .*

○ *To transform my dream into reality, I need to . . .*

_____
_____
_____
_____
_____
_____
_____
_____
_____
_____
_____
_____
_____
_____
_____
_____
_____
_____
_____
_____

AND ELISHA PRAYED, AND SAID, "LORD, I PRAY, OPEN HIS
EYES THAT HE MAY SEE." THEN THE LORD OPENED THE EYES
OF THE YOUNG MAN, AND HE SAW. AND BEHOLD, THE
MOUNTAIN WAS FULL OF CHARIOTS OF FIRE ALL
AROUND ELISHA.

EXODUS 3:16–17

○ Today's opportunities and challenges . . .

   ○ To transform my dream into reality, I need to . . .

AND DO NOT BE
CONFORMED TO
THIS WORLD, BUT
BE TRANSFORMED
BY THE RENEWING
OF YOUR MIND,
THAT YOU MAY
PROVE WHAT IS
THAT GOOD AND
ACCEPTABLE AND
PERFECT WILL OF
GOD.

ROMANS 12:2

Date

○ Today's opportunities and challenges . . .
　　○ To transform my dream into reality, I need to . . .

Perfect faith cannot exist where the will of God is unknown.

Date

○ *Today's opportunities and challenges . . .*

  ○ *To transform my dream into reality, I need to . . .*

THEREFORE DO
NOT CAST AWAY
YOUR CONFIDENCE,
WHICH HAS GREAT
REWARD. FOR YOU
HAVE NEED OF
ENDURANCE, SO
THAT AFTER YOU
HAVE DONE THE
WILL OF GOD, YOU
MAY RECEIVE THE
PROMISE.

HEBREWS 10:35–36

○ *Today's opportunities and challenges . . .*

   ○ *To transform my dream into reality, I need to . . .*

Your situation can take years to catch up with your revelation.

○ Today's opportunities and challenges . . .

   ○ To transform my dream into reality, I need to . . .

MY BRETHREN,
COUNT IT ALL JOY
WHEN YOU FALL INTO
VARIOUS TRIALS,
KNOWING THAT THE
TESTING OF YOUR
FAITH PRODUCES
PATIENCE. BUT LET
PATIENCE HAVE ITS
PERFECT WORK, THAT
YOU MAY BE PERFECT
AND COMPLETE,
LACKING NOTHING.

JAMES 1:2–4

○ Today's opportunities and challenges . . .

   ○ To transform my dream into reality, I need to . . .

Date

○ *Today's opportunities and challenges . . .*

○ *To transform my dream into reality, I need to . . .*

"IF YOU SHOULD SAY
IN YOUR HEART,
'THESE NATIONS ARE
GREATER THAN I; HOW
CAN I DISPOSSESS
THEM?'—YOU SHALL
NOT BE AFRAID OF
THEM, BUT YOU SHALL
REMEMBER WELL WHAT
THE LORD YOUR GOD
DID TO PHARAOH AND
TO ALL EGYPT."

DEUTERONOMY 7:17–18

Date

○ Today's opportunities and challenges . . .

　○ To transform my dream into reality, I need to . . .

Link up with a vision that is bigger than yourself.

Date

○ *Today's opportunities and challenges . . .*

   ○ *To transform my dream into reality, I need to . . .*

THE HIGHWAY OF THE
UPRIGHT IS TO
DEPART FROM EVIL; HE
WHO KEEPS HIS WAY
PRESERVES HIS SOUL.
PRIDE GOES BEFORE
DESTRUCTION, AND A
HAUGHTY SPIRIT
BEFORE A FALL.
BETTER TO BE OF A
HUMBLE SPIRIT WITH
THE LOWLY, THAN TO
DIVIDE THE SPOIL
WITH THE PROUD.

PROVERBS 16:17–19

Date

○ *Today's opportunities and challenges . . .*

    ○ *To transform my dream into reality, I need to . . .*

Don't let your gifting take you where your character can't keep you.

Date

○ *Today's opportunities and challenges . . .*

○ *To transform my dream into reality, I need to . . .*

DEATH AND LIFE
ARE IN THE POWER
OF THE TONGUE,
AND THOSE WHO
LOVE IT WILL EAT
ITS FRUIT.

PROVERBS 18:21

○ Today's opportunities and challenges . . .

　○ To transform my dream into reality, I need to . . .

You frame your world by the words you speak.

○ *Today's opportunities and challenges . . .*

○ *To transform my dream into reality, I need to . . .*

HAVING THEN
GIFTS DIFFERING
ACCORDING TO
THE GRACE THAT
IS GIVEN TO US,
LET US USE THEM:
IF PROPHECY, LET
US PROPHESY IN
PROPORTION TO
OUR FAITH; OR
MINISTRY, LET US
USE IT IN OUR
MINISTERING; HE
WHO TEACHES, IN
TEACHING; HE
WHO EXHORTS, IN
EXHORTATION;
HE WHO GIVES,
WITH LIBERALITY;
HE WHO LEADS,
WITH DILIGENCE;
HE WHO SHOWS
MERCY, WITH
CHEERFULNESS.

ROMANS 12:6–8

Date

○ *Today's opportunities and challenges . . .*

  ○ *To transform my dream into reality, I need to . . .*

It's time to discover new strengths within yourself and build on them to achieve your God-given potential and goals.

Reflections 3

LONG BEFORE David defeated Goliath and ultimately became the King of Israel, he had slain a lion and a bear as he kept his father's sheep. The dreams and the giftings that God has given you develop in obscurity, not notoriety. Be patient and faithful to God as He works in your life. Keep moving forward, and you will not be disappointed.

TAKE TIME TO REVIEW the last several pages of this journal. Reflect on all the things you have discovered about your dreams. As you've thought about your dreams in the light of God's Word, what are you learning? Are there specific dreams that you believe God wants you to focus upon? What can you do to make your dreams come true?

CAPTURE your thoughts below.

....

....

....

....

....

....

....

Date

○ *Today's opportunities and challenges . . .*

   ○ *To transform my dream into reality, I need to . . .*

PRAYING ALWAYS
WITH ALL PRAYER
AND SUPPLICATION
IN THE SPIRIT,
BEING WATCHFUL
TO THIS END WITH
ALL PERSEVERANCE
AND SUPPLICATION
FOR ALL THE
SAINTS.

EPHESIANS 6:18

Date

○ Today's opportunities and challenges . . .

　　○ To transform my dream into reality, I need to . . .

If the enemy can't get you to quit, he will get
you distracted.

Date

○ *Today's opportunities and challenges . . .*

  ○ *To transform my dream into reality, I need to . . .*

FOR I AM THE
LEAST OF THE
APOSTLES, WHO AM
NOT WORTHY TO
BE CALLED AN
APOSTLE, BECAUSE
I PERSECUTED THE
CHURCH OF GOD.
BUT BY THE GRACE
OF GOD I AM
WHAT I AM, AND
HIS GRACE
TOWARD ME WAS
NOT IN VAIN; BUT
I LABORED MORE
ABUNDANTLY
THAN THEY ALL,
YET NOT I, BUT
THE GRACE OF
GOD WHICH WAS
WITH ME.

1 CORINTHIANS
15:9–10

○ *Today's opportunities and challenges . . .*

   ○ *To transform my dream into reality, I need to . . .*

Don't spend a lifetime trying to be what you were not created to be.

○ Today's opportunities and challenges . . .

   ○ To transform my dream into reality, I need to . . .

"YET THEY SEEK ME
DAILY, AND DELIGHT
TO KNOW MY WAYS, AS
A NATION THAT DID
RIGHTEOUSNESS, AND
DID NOT FORSAKE THE
ORDINANCE OF THEIR
GOD. THEY ASK OF ME
THE ORDINANCES OF
JUSTICE; THEY TAKE
DELIGHT IN
APPROACHING GOD."

ISAIAH 58:2

Date

○ Today's opportunities and challenges . . .

　○ To transform my dream into reality, I need to . . .

Successful people do daily what others do occasionally.

◯ _Today's opportunities and challenges . . ._

◯ _To transform my dream into reality, I need to . . ._

"WHY DO YOU
SPEND MONEY FOR
WHAT IS NOT BREAD,
AND YOUR WAGES
FOR WHAT DOES
NOT SATISFY?
LISTEN CAREFULLY
TO ME, AND EAT
WHAT IS GOOD, AND
LET YOUR SOUL
DELIGHT ITSELF IN
ABUNDANCE.
INCLINE YOUR EAR,
AND COME TO ME.
HEAR, AND YOUR
SOUL SHALL LIVE;
AND I WILL MAKE
AN EVERLASTING
COVENANT WITH
YOU—THE SURE
MERCIES OF DAVID."

ISAIAH 55:2–3

Date

○ *Today's opportunities and challenges . . .*

    ○ *To transform my dream into reality, I need to . . .*

There can be no fulfillment where there is no passion.

Date

○ Today's opportunities and challenges . . .

   ○ To transform my dream into reality, I need to . . .

BEING CONFIDENT
OF THIS VERY
THING, THAT HE
WHO HAS BEGUN A
GOOD WORK IN YOU
WILL COMPLETE IT
UNTIL THE DAY OF
JESUS CHRIST.

PHILIPPIANS 1:6–7

Date

○ _Today's opportunities and challenges . . ._
    ○ _To transform my dream into reality, I need to . . ._

The big four confidence destroyers the devil uses are: anxiety, depression, guilt, and anger.

○ Today's opportunities and challenges . . .

   ○ To transform my dream into reality, I need to . . .

"FOR THE LORD
DOES NOT SEE AS
MAN SEES; FOR
MAN LOOKS AT
THE OUTWARD
APPEARANCE, BUT
THE LORD LOOKS
AT THE HEART."

1 SAMUEL 16:7

Date

○ *Today's opportunities and challenges . . .*

   ○ *To transform my dream into reality, I need to . . .*

Don't let life falsely label you. God will make you "larger than life."

○ Today's opportunities and challenges . . .

   ○ To transform my dream into reality, I need to . . .

"BRING MY SONS
FROM AFAR, AND
MY DAUGHTERS
FROM THE ENDS OF
THE EARTH—
EVERYONE WHO IS
CALLED BY MY
NAME, WHOM I
HAVE CREATED FOR
MY GLORY; I HAVE
FORMED HIM, YES,
I HAVE MADE HIM."

ISAIAH 43:6–7

○ Today's opportunities and challenges . . .

  ○ To transform my dream into reality, I need to . . .

○ *Today's opportunities and challenges . . .*

○ *To transform my dream into reality, I need to . . .*

MY SON, LET THEM
NOT DEPART FROM
YOUR EYES—KEEP
SOUND WISDOM
AND DISCRETION;
SO THEY WILL BE
LIFE TO YOUR
SOUL AND GRACE
TO YOUR NECK.
THEN YOU WILL
WALK SAFELY IN
YOUR WAY, AND
YOUR FOOT WILL
NOT STUMBLE.

PROVERBS 3:21—23

Date ....

○ Today's opportunities and challenges . . .

   ○ To transform my dream into reality, I need to . . .

_____

_____

_____

_____

_____

_____

_____

_____

_____

_____

_____

_____

_____

_____

_____

_____

_____

_____

_____

_____

_____

_____

Depreciation occurs when you fail to invest in yourself.

Date ....

○ Today's opportunities and challenges . . .

   ○ To transform my dream into reality, I need to . . .

"FOR THE VISION
IS YET FOR AN
APPOINTED TIME;
BUT AT THE END
IT WILL SPEAK,
AND IT WILL NOT
LIE. THOUGH IT
TARRIES, WAIT
FOR IT; BECAUSE
IT WILL SURELY
COME, IT WILL
NOT TARRY."

HABAKKUK 2:3

Date

○ Today's opportunities and challenges . . .

   ○ To transform my dream into reality, I need to . . .

Build an ark and let the rain catch up to your vision.

○ *Today's opportunities and challenges . . .*

   ○ *To transform my dream into reality, I need to . . .*

SO MOSES'
FATHER-IN-LAW
SAID TO HIM, "THE
THING THAT YOU
DO IS NOT GOOD.
BOTH YOU AND
THESE PEOPLE
WHO ARE WITH
YOU WILL SURELY
WEAR YOURSELVES
OUT. FOR THIS
THING IS TOO
MUCH FOR YOU;
YOU ARE NOT ABLE
TO PERFORM IT BY
YOURSELF. LISTEN
NOW TO MY VOICE;
I WILL GIVE YOU
COUNSEL, AND
GOD WILL BE
WITH YOU."

EXODUS 18:17–19

Date

○ Today's opportunities and challenges . . .

   ○ To transform my dream into reality, I need to . . .

Anyone can be more creative. It starts by looking for new solutions...by not being satisfied with the first answer you come up with.

Date

○ *Today's opportunities and challenges . . .*

 ○ *To transform my dream into reality, I need to . . .*

THEN JOB
ANSWERED THE
LORD AND SAID:
"I KNOW THAT
YOU CAN DO
EVERYTHING,
AND THAT NO
PURPOSE OF
YOURS CAN BE
WITHHELD FROM
YOU."

JOB 42:1–2

○ Today's opportunities and challenges . . .

   ○ To transform my dream into reality, I need to . . .

Don't limit yourself by staying within the perimeters. Think outside of the box.

Date

○ *Today's opportunities and challenges . . .*

  ○ *To transform my dream into reality, I need to . . .*

AND LET US CONSIDER
ONE ANOTHER IN
ORDER TO STIR UP
LOVE AND GOOD
WORKS, NOT FORSAK-
ING THE ASSEMBLING
OF OURSELVES
TOGETHER, AS IS THE
MANNER OF SOME, BUT
EXHORTING ONE
ANOTHER, AND SO
MUCH THE MORE AS
YOU SEE THE DAY
APPROACHING.

HEBREWS 10:24–25

Date

○ *Today's opportunities and challenges . . .*

　○ *To transform my dream into reality, I need to . . .*

Find people who enhance you rather than inhibit you.

Date

◯ *Today's opportunities and challenges . . .*

   ◯ *To transform my dream into reality, I need to . . .*

BUT TO EACH ONE
OF US GRACE WAS
GIVEN ACCORDING
TO THE MEASURE
OF CHRIST'S GIFT.

EPHESIANS 4:7

○ *Today's opportunities and challenges . . .*

　　○ *To transform my dream into reality, I need to . . .*

You are filled with endless potential and possibilities.

○ *Today's opportunities and challenges . . .*

THEN KING NEBUCHADNEZZAR FELL ON HIS FACE, PROSTRATE
BEFORE DANIEL, AND COMMANDED THAT THEY SHOULD
PRESENT AN OFFERING AND INCENSE TO HIM. THE KING
ANSWERED DANIEL, AND SAID, "TRULY YOUR GOD IS THE GOD
OF GODS, THE LORD OF KINGS, AND A REVEALER OF SECRETS,
SINCE YOU COULD REVEAL THIS SECRET." THEN THE KING
PROMOTED DANIEL AND GAVE HIM MANY GREAT GIFTS; AND HE
MADE HIM RULER OVER THE WHOLE PROVINCE OF BABYLON, AND
CHIEF ADMINISTRATOR OVER ALL THE WISE MEN OF BABYLON.

DANIEL 2:46–48

○ *To transform my dream into reality, I need to . . .*

Date

○ *Today's opportunities and challenges . . .*

   ○ *To transform my dream into reality, I need to . . .*

"BRING ALL THE
TITHES INTO THE
STOREHOUSE, THAT
THERE MAY BE
FOOD IN MY
HOUSE, AND TRY
ME NOW IN THIS,"
SAYS THE LORD OF
HOSTS, "IF I WILL
NOT OPEN FOR YOU
THE WINDOWS OF
HEAVEN AND POUR
OUT FOR YOU SUCH
BLESSING THAT
THERE WILL NOT BE
ROOM ENOUGH TO
RECEIVE IT."

MALACHI 3:10

Date

○ Today's opportunities and challenges . . .

   ○ To transform my dream into reality, I need to . . .

Initiate your blessing. Nothing significant will happen until you initiate it.

Date

○ Today's opportunities and challenges . . .

○ *To transform my dream into reality, I need to . . .*

_____

_____

_____

_____

_____

_____

_____

God will only promote us as high as our character will take us.

_____

_____

_____

_____

_____

_____

_____

_____

_____

_____

_____

_____

○ *Today's opportunities and challenges* . . .

   ○ *To transform my dream into reality, I need to* . . .

BUT RUTH SAID:
"ENTREAT ME NOT
TO LEAVE YOU, OR
TO TURN BACK
FROM FOLLOWING
AFTER YOU; FOR
WHEREVER YOU GO,
I WILL GO; AND
WHEREVER YOU
LODGE, I WILL
LODGE; YOUR PEO-
PLE SHALL BE MY
PEOPLE, AND YOUR
GOD, MY GOD.
WHERE YOU DIE, I
WILL DIE, AND
THERE WILL I BE
BURIED. THE LORD
DO SO TO ME, AND
MORE ALSO, IF
ANYTHING BUT
DEATH PARTS YOU
AND ME."

RUTH 1:16–17

Date

○ Today's opportunities and challenges . . .

  ○ To transform my dream into reality, I need to . . .

_____

_____

_____

_____

_____

_____

Challenge yourself out of your comfort zone and into your commitment zone.

_____

_____

_____

_____

_____

_____

_____

_____

_____

_____

_____

Date

○ _Today's opportunities and challenges..._

　　○ _To transform my dream into reality, I need to..._

FOR DO I NOW
PERSUADE MEN, OR
GOD? OR DO I
SEEK TO PLEASE
MEN? FOR IF I
STILL PLEASED
MEN, I WOULD
NOT BE A BOND-
SERVANT OF
CHRIST.

GALATIANS 1:10

Date

○ Today's opportunities and challenges . . .

   ○ To transform my dream into reality, I need to . . .

If you always please man, you will displease God.

Date

○ Today's opportunities and challenges . . .

○ *To transform my dream into reality, I need to . . .*

....

....

....

....

....

If not now, then when? If not you, then who? The only place to start is where you are.

....

....

....

....

....

....

....

....

....

....

....

....

....

Date

○ *Today's opportunities and challenges . . .*

    ○ *To transform my dream into reality, I need to . . .*

NOW THE MAN
MOSES WAS VERY
HUMBLE, MORE
THAN ALL MEN
WHO WERE ON THE
FACE OF THE
EARTH.

NUMBERS 12:3

Date

○ Today's opportunities and challenges . . .

  ○ To transform my dream into reality, I need to . . .

You can have excellence without arrogance.

Date

○ Today's opportunities and challenges . . .

○ To transform my dream into reality, I need to . . .

"ONLY TAKE HEED
TO YOURSELF, AND
DILIGENTLY KEEP
YOURSELF, LEST
YOU FORGET THE
THINGS YOUR EYES
HAVE SEEN, AND
LEST THEY DEPART
FROM YOUR HEART
ALL THE DAYS OF
YOUR LIFE."

DEUTERONOMY 4:9

Date

○ Today's opportunities and challenges . . .

   ○ To transform my dream into reality, I need to . . .

In your hour of elevation, don't forget God.

Date ....

○ *Today's opportunities and challenges . . .*

  ○ *To transform my dream into reality, I need to . . .*

"EYE HAS NOT SEEN,
NOR EAR HEARD,
NOR HAVE ENTERED
INTO THE HEART
OF MAN THE
THINGS WHICH
GOD HAS PREPARED
FOR THOSE WHO
LOVE HIM." BUT
GOD HAS REVEALED
THEM TO US
THROUGH HIS
SPIRIT. FOR THE
SPIRIT SEARCHES
ALL THINGS, YES,
THE DEEP THINGS
OF GOD.

I CORINTHIANS 2:9—10

Date

○ Today's opportunities and challenges . . .

   ○ To transform my dream into reality, I need to . . .

Build a dream beyond your means.

Date

◯ Today's opportunities and challenges . . .

○ *To transform my dream into reality, I need to . . .*

AND MORDECAI TOLD THEM TO ANSWER ESTHER:
"DO NOT THINK IN YOUR HEART THAT YOU WILL ESCAPE
IN THE KING'S PALACE ANY MORE THAN ALL THE OTHER
JEWS. FOR IF YOU REMAIN COMPLETELY SILENT AT THIS
TIME, RELIEF AND DELIVERANCE WILL ARISE FOR THE JEWS
FROM ANOTHER PLACE, BUT YOU AND YOUR FATHER'S
HOUSE WILL PERISH. YET WHO KNOWS WHETHER YOU
HAVE COME TO THE KINGDOM FOR SUCH A TIME AS THIS?"

ESTHER 4:13–14

○ Today's opportunities and challenges . . .

　○ To transform my dream into reality, I need to . . .

"HEAR, O ISRAEL:
TODAY YOU ARE
ON THE VERGE OF
BATTLE WITH
YOUR ENEMIES. DO
NOT LET YOUR
HEART FAINT, DO
NOT BE AFRAID,
AND DO NOT
TREMBLE OR BE
TERRIFIED
BECAUSE OF THEM;
FOR THE LORD
YOUR GOD IS HE
WHO GOES WITH
YOU, TO FIGHT
FOR YOU AGAINST
YOUR ENEMIES, TO
SAVE YOU."

DEUTERONOMY 20:3–4

Date

○ *Today's opportunities and challenges . . .*

  ○ *To transform my dream into reality, I need to . . .*

You don't conquer without conflict. You don't win without war.

◯ Today's opportunities and challenges . . .

  ◯ To transform my dream into reality, I need to . . .

FINALLY, MY
BRETHREN, BE
STRONG IN THE
LORD AND IN THE
POWER OF HIS
MIGHT.

EPHESIANS 6:10

Date

○ Today's opportunities and challenges . . .

    ○ To transform my dream into reality, I need to . . .

You cannot birth the promise effectively if you are "weak" in self!

Date

○ *Today's opportunities and challenges . . .*

○ *To transform my dream into reality, I need to . . .*

THE RIGHTEOUS
SHOULD CHOOSE
HIS FRIENDS CARE-
FULLY, FOR THE WAY
OF THE WICKED
LEADS THEM
ASTRAY.

PROVERBS 12:26

Date

○ *Today's opportunities and challenges . . .*

　　○ *To transform my dream into reality, I need to . . .*

No one becomes successful by accident.

Date

○ *Today's opportunities and challenges . . .*

  ○ *To transform my dream into reality, I need to . . .*

"I HAVE COME
THAT THEY MAY
HAVE LIFE, AND
THAT THEY MAY
HAVE IT MORE
ABUNDANTLY."

JOHN 10:10

Date

○ Today's opportunities and challenges . . .

   ○ To transform my dream into reality, I need to . . .

You must "think big" to do God-sized things.

Date

○ _Today's opportunities and challenges . . ._

   ○ _To transform my dream into reality, I need to . . ._

DO NOT BE
DECEIVED: "EVIL
COMPANY CORRUPTS
GOOD HABITS."

1 CORINTHIANS 15:33

Date

○ Today's opportunities and challenges . . .

  ○ To transform my dream into reality, I need to . . .

People either add, subtract, multiply, or divide in your life.

Reflections 4

IF GOD COULD CREATE the worlds we see by His word alone, "so that the things which are seen were not made of things which are visible" (Hebrews 11:3), He can easily help you give birth to your dreams. While you are waiting, the makings of a miracle are growing inside of you. Never give up on yourself. Live in the "yes" zone—"yes, I trust you, Lord, to make my dreams real."

TAKE TIME TO REVIEW the last several pages of this journal. Reflect on all the things you have discovered about your dreams. As you've thought about your dreams in the light of God's Word, what are you learning? Are there specific dreams that you believe God wants you to focus upon? What can you do to make your dreams come true?

CAPTURE your thoughts below.

....

....

....

....

....

Date

Reflections 4 continued...

Thoughts and Notes